The Art of Newborn Photography

Hector M. Melendez

Copyright © 2020 Hector M. Melendez All rights reserved

No part of this book may be reproduced, or stored in a retrieval system, or transmitted in any form or by any means, electronic, mechanical, photocopying, recording, or otherwise, without express written permission of the publisher.

Printed in the United States of America

CONTENTS

Title Page

Copyright

Introduction

Important Message

Information for Parents

Our Preparation

Parent Preparation

Light

Posing

Details

Family Photos

Tips for Taking Great Pictures

Equipment

Contingency Planning

Editing

Final Product

INTRODUCTION

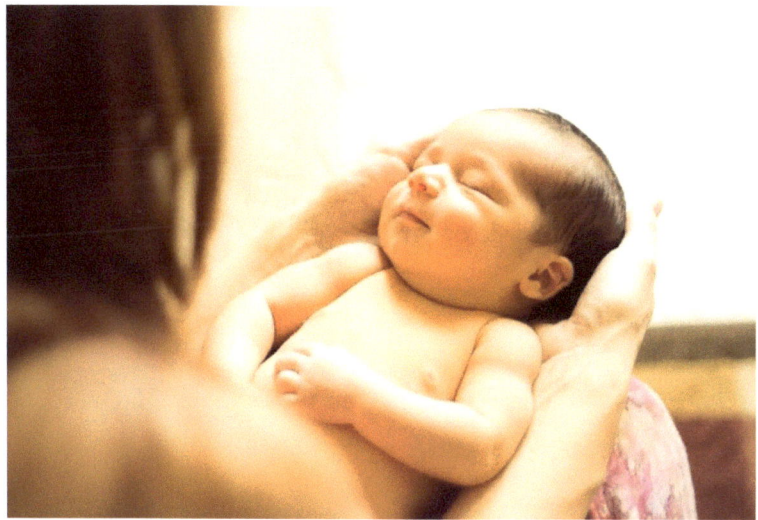

My interest in photography began with landscapes. Being a resident of the Caribbean island of Puerto Rico and having as many beautiful landscapes as beaches, tropical forests, rivers, and mountains, helped me develop my eye for this art. It was not until the birth of my first child that I entered the world of newborn photography, my children being the best motivation to read books, take courses and practice. I decided to practice with my friends' babies and in a short time I began to be referred to work for other people, this being my starting point in the photography business. In this book I share my techniques for taking great pictures of newborns. This book is intended for people with a basic understanding of photography. I recommend that people who are starting to use a DSLR camera to buy a basic photography book and learn first how to use their camera in manual mode. I hope you enjoy and learn by reading this book and start taking great pictures.

IMPORTANT MESSAGE

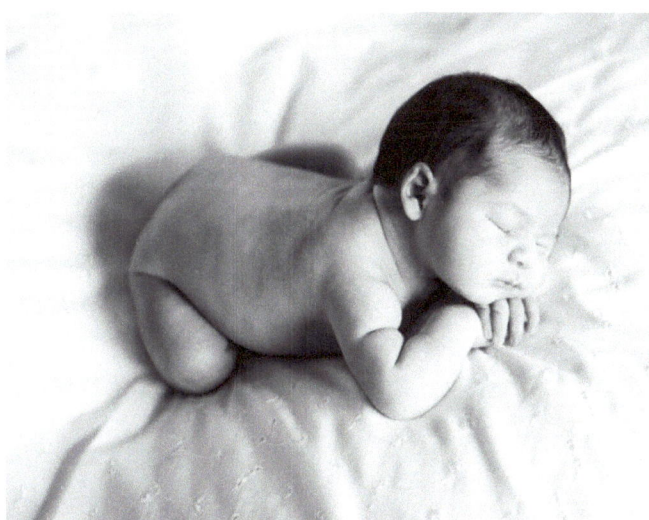

As newborn photographers we must bear in mind that we are going to work with babies no more than two weeks old. Therefore, we must have basic knowledge of handling babies of this age. This knowledge is necessary for the handling of the newborn regarding the poses necessary for a successful session and for the safety of the baby. If we do not have this knowledge, we must somehow acquire it before we can work as newborn photographers.

INFORMATION FOR PARENTS

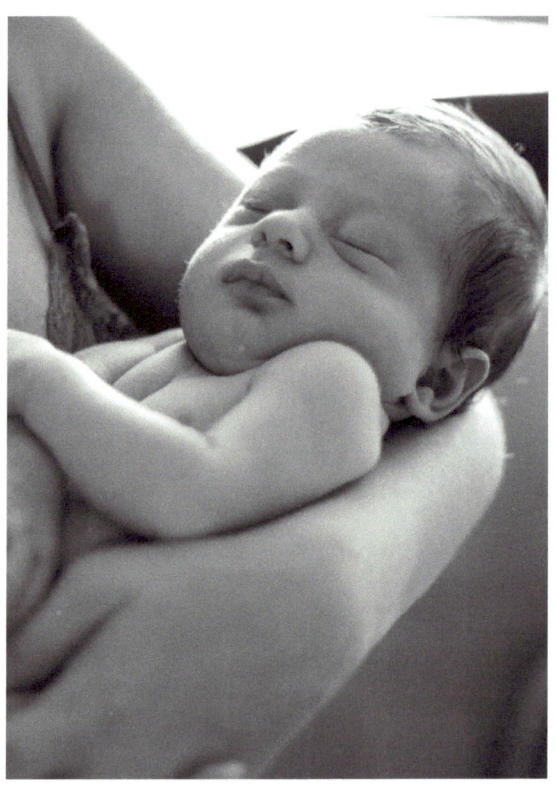

Usually the hiring of our services as photographers can be during the pregnancy photo shoot, when there are still several months before birth. At this time, we must inform parents that the newborn session should be coordinated before the baby is two weeks old. This is of utmost importance, as babies are not as manageable after these two weeks. They do not fall asleep; they do not hold their poses and we can have a very frustrating session.

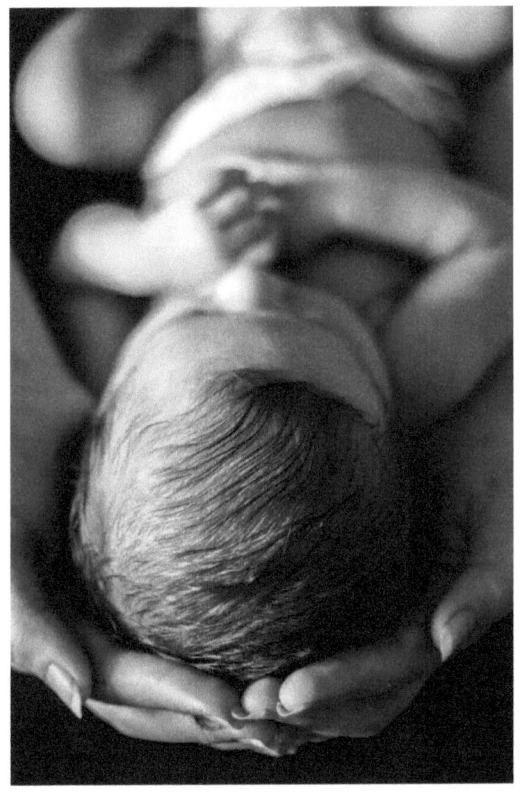

When the parents call me to coordinate a newborn session, I ask if they are more than two weeks old. If the answer is yes, I explain to the parents the risk involved. Remember that parents' expectations are high for the final product of the session, and our reputation as photographers is at risk when we agree to work in a difficult session.

OUR PREPARATION

Preparation for a newborn session is of utmost importance. We must have on hand a checklist for each of our sessions so that we do not miss anything. Remember that accidents are inevitable, so you 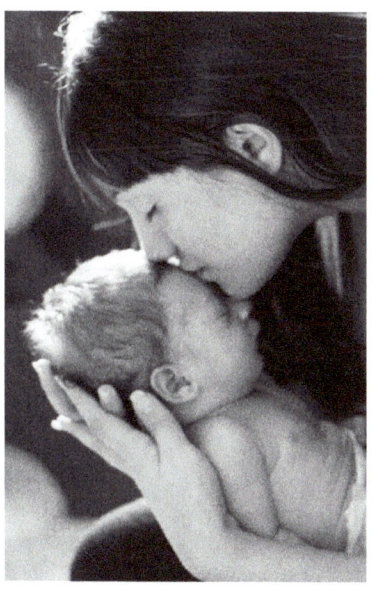 must be prepared for everything. In this chapter I list the essential items we should have on hand:

- Special portable bed for posing newborns
- Waterproof cover for the portable bed
- At least four towels

- At least three thick sheets in solid colors to put the baby to portable bed (washed with hypoallergenic detergent)
- Hand sanitizer
- Baby wipes

It is important to emphasize in the case that we are male photographers and the session is for a baby girl, I recommend that we have a female assistant to have more confidence from the parents.

PARENT PREPARATION

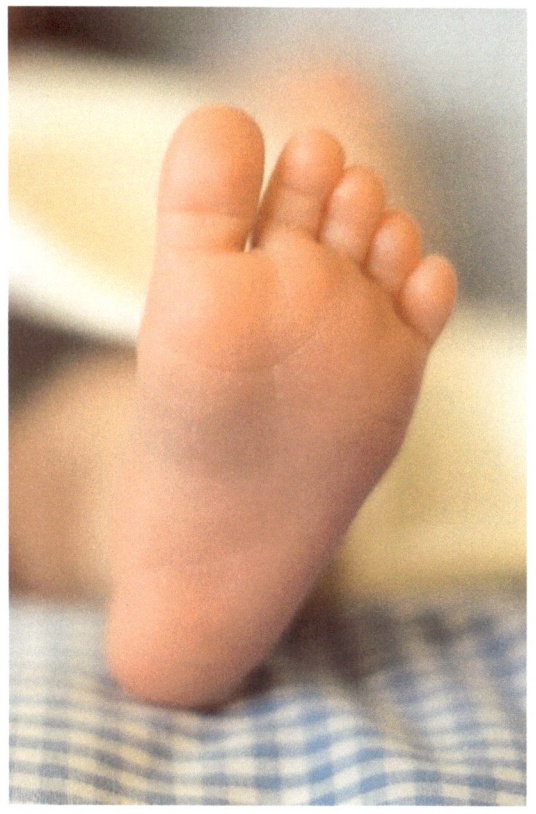

Communication is important. Days before the session, we should talk to parents, so they know how to be prepared. The time of the photographer's arrival must be well coordinated since the baby must have his full tummy by then. This is necessary so that they remain asleep during the first hours of the session. It is important that you select a spacious room with plenty of natural light. The house should be as quiet as possible. There should be no unnecessary noise. Since the baby is going to be naked in some moments it is important that the air conditioners are not turned on. The room must have a warm temperature so that the baby remains asleep. Parents should have on hand all the items with which they want their babies to look in the session, such as hats, ties, etc. If parents have plans to participate in the session, we must remind them to be prepared with their clothing. Comfortable clothing and solid colors are ideal.

LIGHT

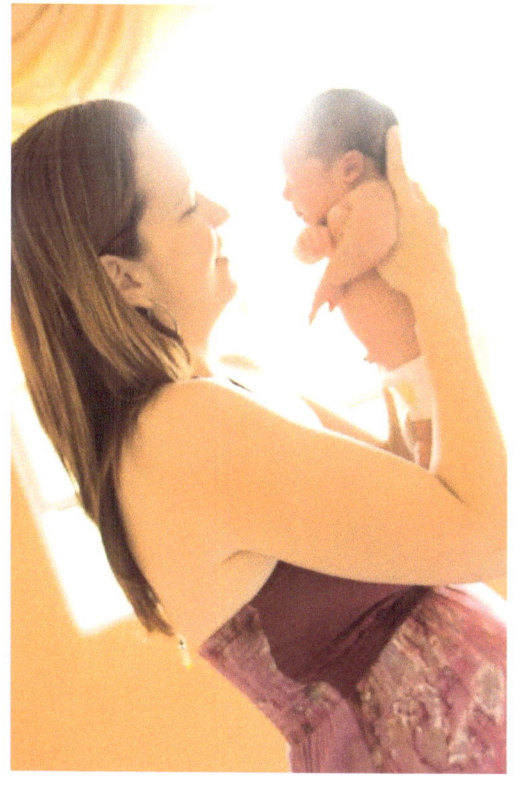

I carry out my newborn sessions in the residences of my clients. Because newborn sessions are held indoors, we must keep in mind that we need good lighting. We should use the most illuminated room in the residence. If we do not have enough light, we need to complement with artificial light by means of external flash. If we have natural light, we must use it to our advantage. We must accommodate babies so that their faces are illuminated by the light that enters from the window.

We can also use the light from the windows to create a silhouette with a mother holding the baby.

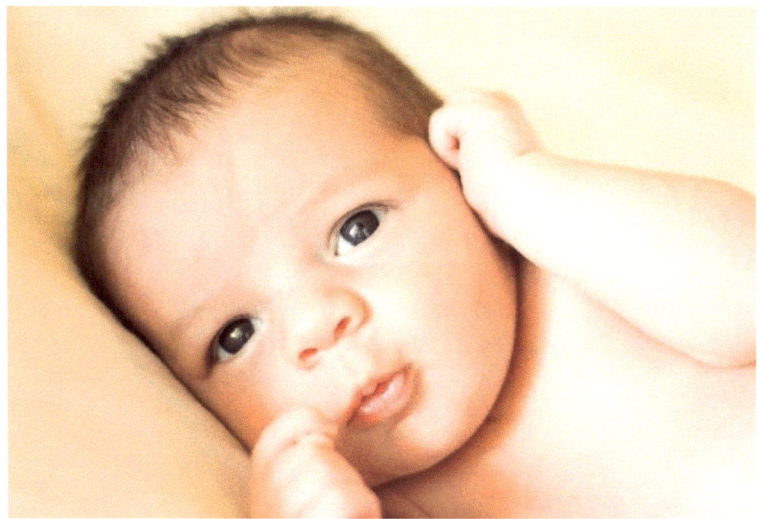

Newborn sessions can take around three hours so it is necessary to calculate the time that we are going to end to make sure that we will have enough natural light during the session.

POSING

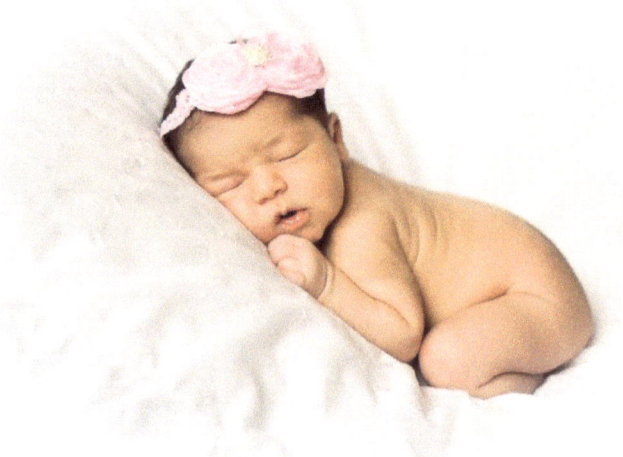

Babies must be asleep to pose them. We will ensure that they always look in a comfortable position. The best position for the legs is the fetal position. This pose is natural for them because in this way they spent a long time inside their mother's belly, and it also looks particularly good in the photo.

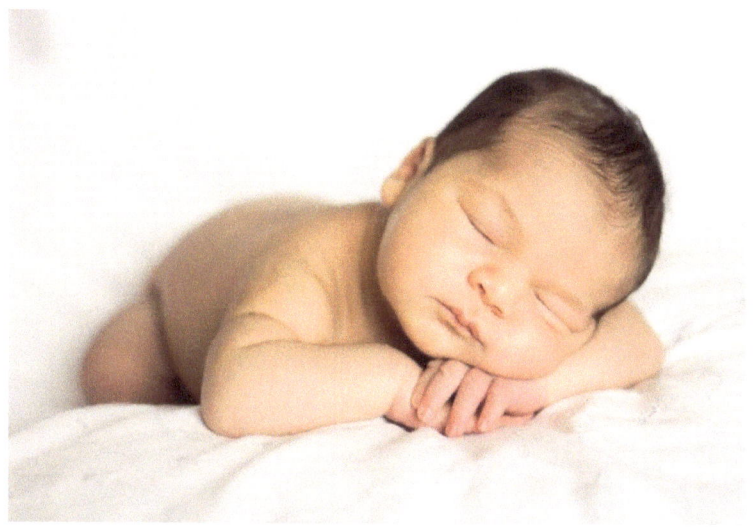

Let us put the hands in a position that does not obstruct the vision of their face. The images in this book have many examples of how we can pose them, and we must vary to obtain different images. Remember that we can take several angles of the same pose to vary.

DETAILS

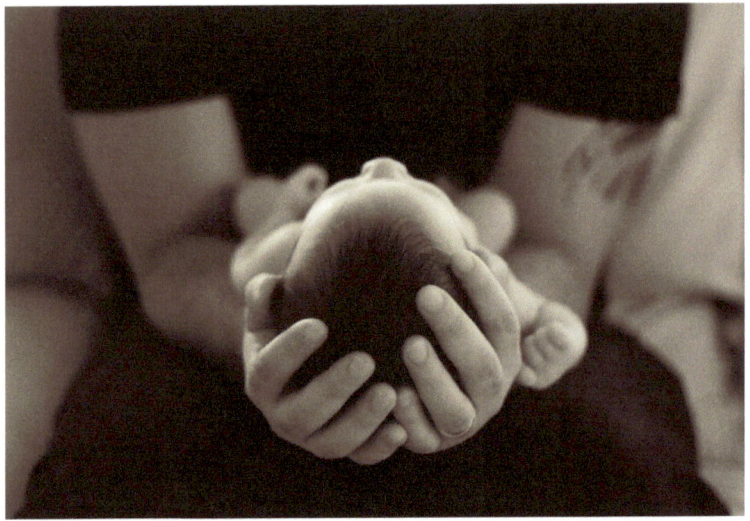

In my opinion, it is necessary to take some details in our newborn sessions. And what better time than when babies are awake. This is the best time to take advantage. Let us take photos of their feet, hands, and face with their eyes open.

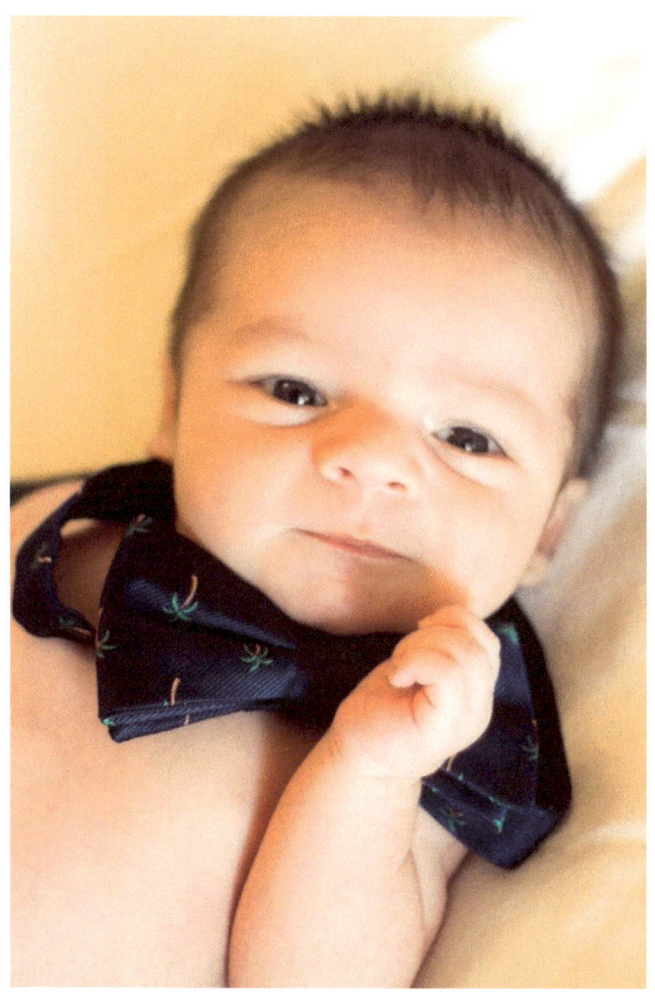

Sometimes it might even seem like they are posing for the camera. Also, the details with the hands of dad or mom can look very artistic.

FAMILY PHOTOS

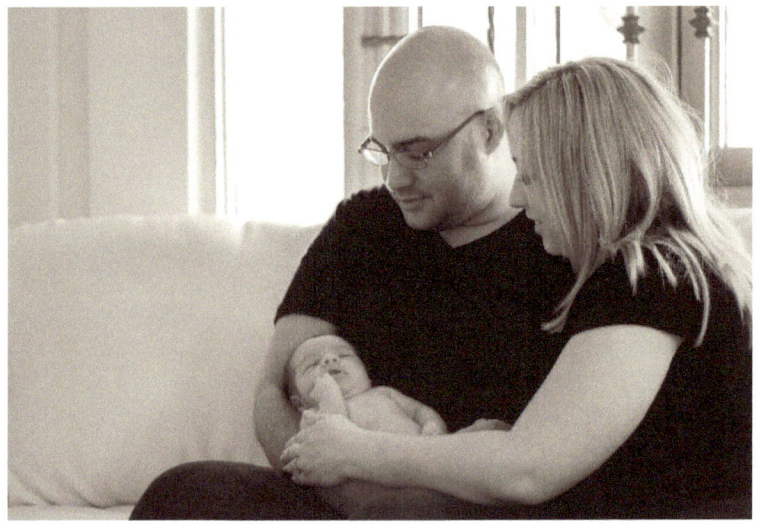

When dad and mom want to be part of the session, we are going to do it in an artistic way. We can look for different corners of the house to be creative and look for good angles. We are going to use the light that comes in from the windows to our advantage.

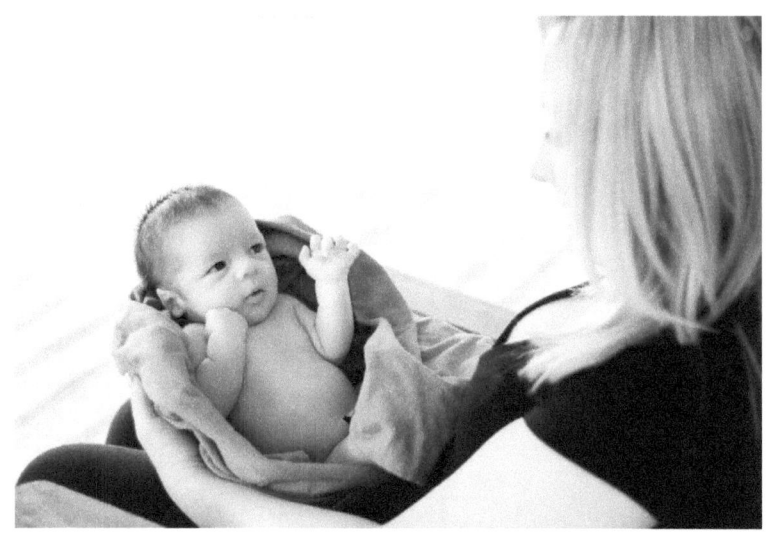

Mama in the rocking chair can look very charming.

TIPS FOR TAKING GREAT PICTURES

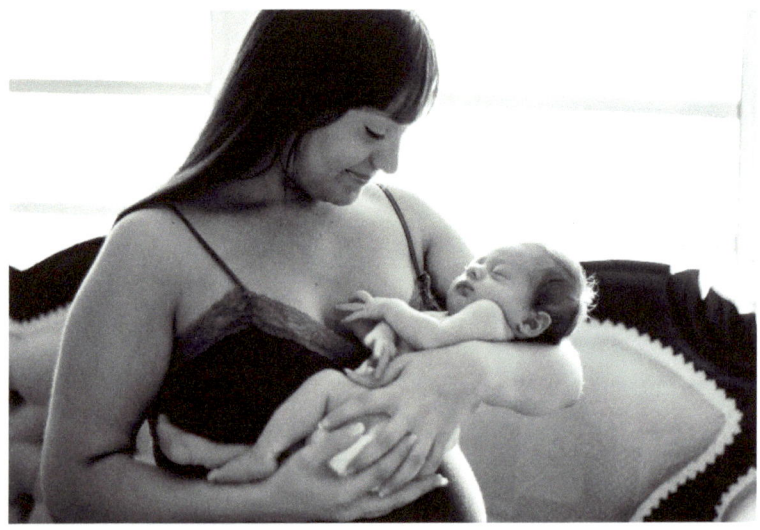

Let us always focus the camera on the eyes of our subjects. Let us always work with the camera in burst mode. In this way we try not to miss the perfect moment. We should never be concerned about running out of memory. These days memory cards are cheap. Let us buy memory cards with enough space and always have a card for backup. It is important that our images look clean. There should be the least number of objects that distract the viewer's eye.

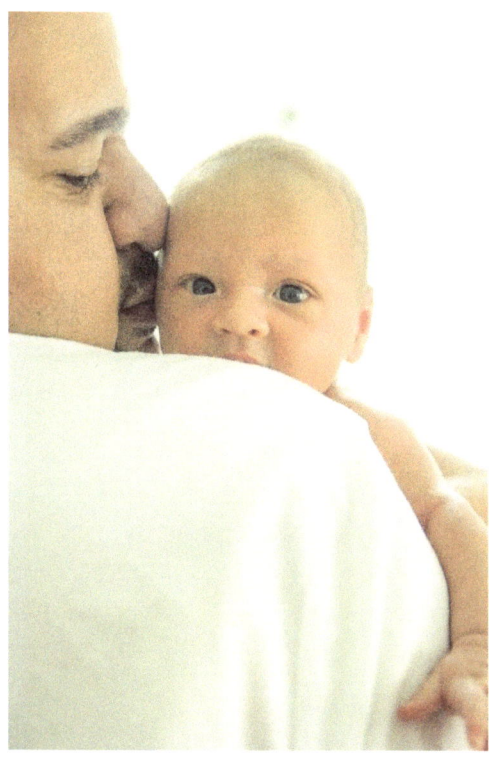

There should be no other people than our subjects. It should appear that our subjects are alone in the photo. So, blurring the background is important. This makes our subjects the main character. Less is more. Let us use the spot meter in our camera to measure light with a neutral color. Let us consider the light changes and re-measure if necessary. Always be ready for the moment, with both hands on the camera. Let us compose with our eye carefully and take the images. In this way we avoid spending more time editing. Remember that cropping too much reduces the resolution of the image.

EQUIPMENT

- Two DSLR cameras
- Telephoto Lens 28-70mm (for camera with full-size sensor) or 17-50mm (for camera with APS-C sensor) with 2.8 maximum aperture at any distance and image stabilization
- Normal lens 50mm with maximum aperture of 1.8 or 1.4
- Battery grip for more power time and better camera handling
- External flash
- Two memory cards with space for at least 1,000 images each
- Tripod- Lens cleaning kit
- Lens hood
- Camera equipment bag

CONTINGENCY PLANNING

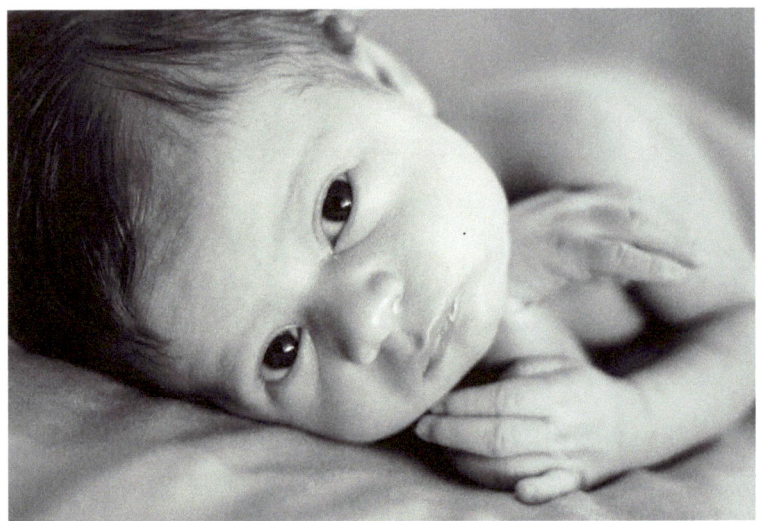

Backing up to a computer, external drive, and a cloud service the same day as the session is a must. When editing, let us back up your work every day. In this way we avoid losing our work in the event of any accident.

EDITING

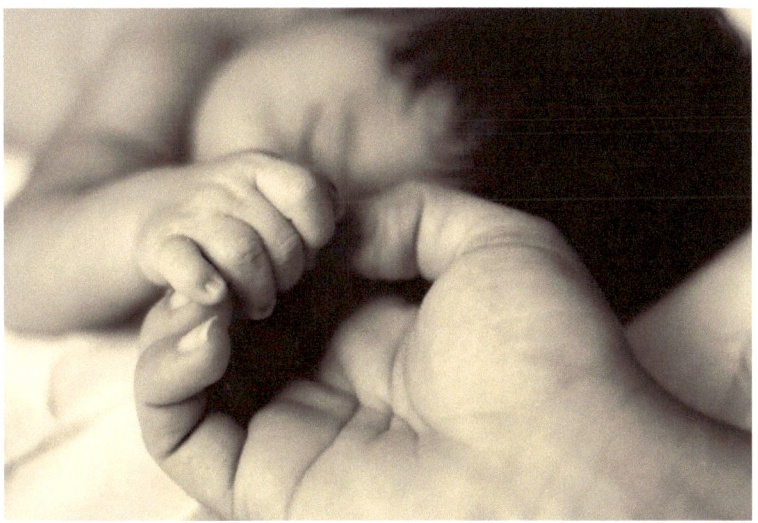

My advice is to take all our photos in RAW format. This way we will have more control when editing. We can crop, adjust white balance, move up or down up to two full stops in case we lose the correct exposure due to light changes, and we can adjust shadows, reflections, and colors. The photos in jpeg format are not very manageable. Use a good computer application to handle the RAW photo format. After we finish editing, we convert to the jpeg format for the final product.

FINAL PRODUCT

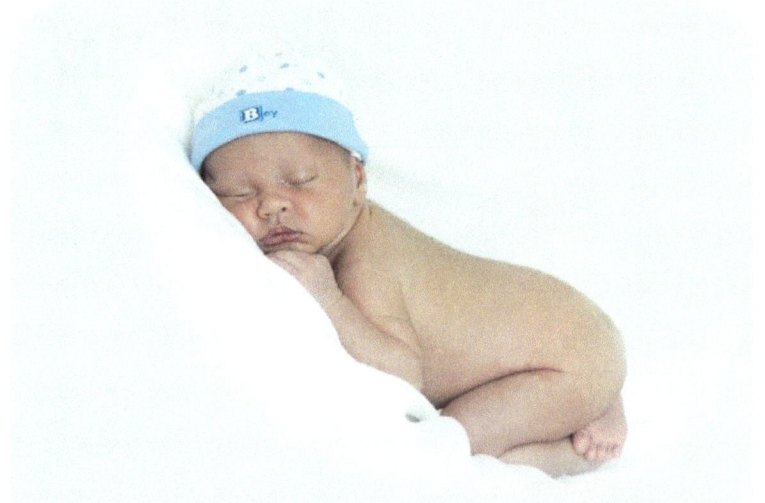

Because in newborn sessions I always work with my camera in burst mode, I can end up with around 200 photos per session. Already sitting in front of my computer, I start to select the photos that artistically meet my requirements, and then I start editing. I deliver about 35 color images with black and white copies, on a well-presented device. On the Internet we can find several photography companies that help us with interesting articles and quality devices to store photos.

www.ingramcontent.com/pod-product-compliance
Lightning Source LLC
Chambersburg PA
CBHW041949240526
45473CB00036B/2796